SPIRITUAL AWAKENING

A BEGINNER'S GUIDE TO SPIRITUAL ALCHEMY

JESSICA MCRAE

SPIRITUAL AWAKENING
A BEGINNER'S GUIDE TO SPIRITUAL ALCHEMY

Spiritual Alchemy is intensely spiritual and deeply personal, but if you mindfully follow each stage applying them to yourself you will find yourself healed from your past traumas and fear, renewed in spirit, and have found a deep understanding of yourself.

As you read this book, don't be surprised to find you have experienced one or more stages already. In practicing the stages of alchemy, I encourage you to incorporate them into your spiritual practice. It is advised you should achieve a solitude meditative state prior to commencing in alchemical work.

Practice often by quieting your mind, identifying negative thoughts arising and choose again pushing the negativity away from you. Always use your divine intuition and direction from God, Angels, and your spirit guides. Intentionally bring in beautiful God energy and let it flow through you.

I wish you love and peace!

Table Of Contents

PREFACE

The goals of this series are the reawakening of our inherent healing powers and our transformation into a higher awareness of our potential to navigate the mysteries of this miraculous life. Spiritual Alchemy is both a school of knowledge and a spiritual path to an enlightened state of presence.

You will understand the depth of the 3 realms of Spiritual Alchemy:

Nigredo (Dark Night of the Soul)
Albedo (Purification and Raising)
Rubedo (Solidify Back into Oneness)

The basic tenets of alchemy can be applied repeatedly in each stage until you have mastered each aspect of yourself at a time.

Your journey into awakened spirituality will come to a full cycle of completion as you gain a deeper understanding of yourself, your souls' journey, and your path to enlightenment.

Spiritual Alchemy is intensely spiritual and deeply personal, so take your time and really invest in yourself.

CHAPTER 1
The Basics

What is alchemy?

We are making the impure pure.

A more technical definition...

The purification of metals, substances, the conscious and subconscious mind, the physical body, and the soul.

Spiritual Definition

Spiritual Alchemy will transform you spiritually, emotionally, and physically but if we look at alchemy as a general term we will see it is applied in many different ways such as chemically... turning base metals like lead and copper into silver or gold, spiritually where you spiritually move from darkness to light or shamanic alchemy where you would do binding of soul activities. There are many more, these a just a few.

Spiritual Alchemy is believing you are whole and also integrating yourself in oneness, refusing to believe in separation. Alchemy is an integration of all aspects of you so that you understand you are perfect and whole.

Alchemy's 1st Law of Equivalent Exchange says humankind cannot gain anything without first giving something in return. To obtain this, something of equal or less value must be lost.

What would you want to shed and gain?

In spiritual alchemy, you will focus on freeing yourself from fears, limiting belief systems, or lack of acceptance and gain the art of transformation through inner liberation, transformation, and change. You will gain a deeper understanding of yourself and a closer connection to God.

In your lifetimes you may only complete 1 or 2 stages, and that's OK. We are students here to learn, remember?

Most people never achieve the alchemical stages to completion unless you are Buddha or Jesus. This all depends on where you are at in your karmic learning as well. It takes a lifetime, even lifetimes, to clear every alloyed aspect of us and then change it to a pure state.

Why does this seem so difficult?

You have free will. You are constantly being presented with lessons that cause you to experience life at various degrees and then process it as a human.

Good news...everyone is different, and every journey is unique.

THE EGYPTIANS MADE IT A SCIENCE

The goals of alchemy in ancient Egyptian practice were to reawaken intrinsic healing powers and transform into a higher awareness of the potential to navigate the lessons of life.

Egyptian alchemy is both a school of knowledge and a spiritual path to an enlightened state of presence.

The basic tenets of alchemy are distilled in the Emerald Tablet, one of the most studied guiding documents of alchemical traditions.

The Emerald Tablet is attributed to Hermes Trismegistus, the legendary author of works on theosophy, magic, wisdom, and alchemy, who is associated with the Greek god Hermes, and the ancient Egyptian god of wisdom, Thoth.

The Tablet suggests that which is above is the same as that which is below: All that exists is of One Mind or One Thing, and they are the same.

This also describes duality.

Life on Earth is like a BIG classroom for your soul.

Did you know your soul ages?

It goes from infancy to maturity just like your body does...except your soul doesn't die, instead, it ages through time through wisdom gained through multiple lifetimes of positive and negative experiences.

How does your soul grow in wisdom?

To learn we must go through the duality of life, experience the male and female, rich and poor, victim and perpetrator, light and dark aspects of self, etc.

As you swing from one side to another you notice one side is pure and innocent, while the other side is ego driven and self-important which keeps you in a state of constantly seeking love. In every moment we constantly swing to both sides with the intent to overcome conditions of the human ego to achieve balance, acceptance, and love.

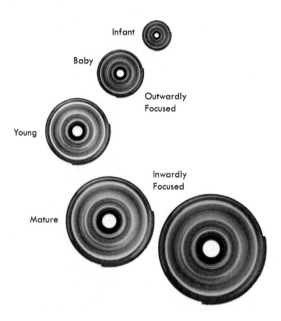

CHAPTER 2
Duality

To understand duality, you must experience the negative to appreciate the positive.

The law of duality states that everything is on a continuum, but has a complimentary opposite within the whole. You may have heard the phrase - the flip side of the coin. On the physical level, the spiritual law of duality is simple to understand because we can easily see and touch a tangible object knowing if something different. One side of the coin is "heads", the other "tails", but both are the same coin.

As humans, we like to label things, to judge them as right or wrong, good or bad. Rather than choose to see experiences as one degree or other, we allow the experience to show what direction is for the highest potential of our soul. We've all had experiences that initially proved unpleasant, but they became the greatest thing that happened to us. Without the positive, we wouldn't appreciate the negative, and vice versa.

If you are only able to see things from one perspective, then you have conditioned yourself to stay within a limited belief system. It is not about operating in either extreme of the spectrum, but rather seeking harmony in both. There's only a source of love that is in perfect alignment with your soul, and when in alignment on a soul level we become in alignment as a collective.

Within the law of duality you may find when you attempt to stay centered, within duality the opposite of what you want will manifest because duality always sets up the energy of conflict.

If you work on changing your thinking and stay neutral, you will reach a point of harmony centered within yourself. Pure innocent love has no balance or depth to it, therefore it's not wise or expansive. Innocent love is like that of a child that has not experienced the corruption of ego and jaded it with status, power, and a need for acceptance from others...it's missing the love from within.

Suppose the innocent love soul can move into the human-conditioned ego soul to find love through the ego experiences such as fear and hardship. In that case, it can swing to a state of balance and exist as wise, healthy unconditional love because it has experienced LIFE conditioning.

CHAPTER 3
The Power of 3

To truly understand spiritual alchemy, you must
understand the power of 3

*"If you only knew the magnificence of the 3, 6,and 9 then you
would have the keys to the universe."*
– Nikola Tesla

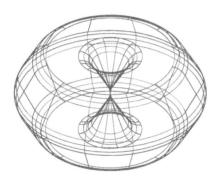

The 3, 6, and 9 represent vectors or energy grids from the 3rd
to the 4th dimensions. A vector is the shape of energy an
object takes as it vibrates...like water when poured is fluid, but
you see it.

It takes on an energy spiral in the 3rd dimension, and 3, 6, and
9 are the vibrational frequencies in the subatomic field known
as the 4th dimension that holds that vector of energy back
together in the 3rd dimension.

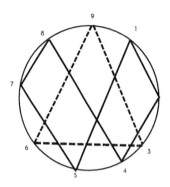

In the vortex to the left, 1,2,4,5,7, and 8 are all connected which represents the physical world, but the numbers 3,6, and 9 hold the vibrational equivalence and hold it back into reality in the 3rd dimension they're located in the 4th dimension (quantum field).

This theory describes the non-physical frequency vibration and energy of physical objects back in 3rd dimension

An atom is 99.999 empty space so notice the nine not to mention that an atom is 99 non-physical but it's manifested as physical so if we apply vector logic, 99.9 % of an atom is invisible energy per the work documented by scientist Marco Rhoden. 369 represents an energy field from the 3rd to 4th dimension. 99.99% of atoms are located in this field of energy outside of the 3rd dimension so clearly the 9 in 99% represents the quantum field. You must think in terms of energy, frequency and vibration.

24 hours/day (4+2=6)

60 minutes/hr (6+0=6)

There is a constant oscillation between 3-6-9.

12, 3, and 6 o'clock

Past - Present - Future

3-6-9 is the basis for Geometry

Geometry circles are 36 degrees
360 degrees

3+6=9

Triangles
the sum of all angles is 180
1+8+0=9

Square
360 degrees
3+6+0=9

DNA

Composed of 3 chemical subunits sequenced three at a time within biological genes and each time you add 3 chemical subunits of DNA you subsequently get 6 and 9 so this is encoded into your DNA and the number 6 3's appear throughout human history

So what does the power of 3 have to do with Spiritual Alchemy?

It's a sacred number.

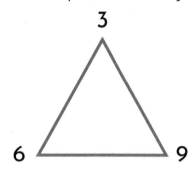

Sacred geometry of the triangle...

The # of spirituality...

The archetype of the father, mother, and child...

The Holy Trinity - Father, Son, Holy Ghost

The Hindu view is that the chakra is part of the esoteric anatomy. They are interconnected with the Nadi which are meridian-like channels that carry energy around the body. Their view proposes that the chakras interface with other energy bodies to assist in the rising of Kundalini (which is a type of live energy that invites a union with the divine).

So, Nadis are channels that flow and interact with the chakra in the physical body. These convey prana, or subtle energy, to cleanse the physical body and invite the Kundalini upward through the chakras - remember Kundalini is a type of live energy that invites a union with the divine. There are 72,000 Nadis but the primary Nadis involved in the kundalini rising are the Ida, which is on the left side of the spine and represents feminine energy; the Pingala, which is on the right side of the spine and signifies male energy; and the Shushma, which is central. in the spine between the Ida and Pingala. As the kundalini rises through the Shushma, the Ida and Pingala coil around the spine at the 7 chakras, activating the chakras, and resulting in a continual rise of the Kundalini.

These subtle energy bodies, the Ida, Pingala, and Shushma, are **three** basic energy bodies that contain the human and spiritual dimensions.

Divine Feminine– ½ of the spirit life - the energy of allowin
trust, faith, and patience that is very loving and nurturing. Th
divine feminine interacts with the world from the heart, a plac
of love feeling freedom from within.

- Mother Gaia
- Moon connection – lunar energy
- Shakti

Divine Masculine – ½ of the spirit life - the energy of logic an
rationality, grounding and creativity. The divine masculin
takes divine feminine energy ideas and puts them into action.

- Hermes
- Sacred Geometry

When the divine feminine and masculine aspects ar
intertwined there lies love, connection with God, nature, an
the collective. We need both to be balanced.

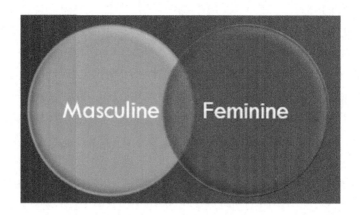

Also within the Triunity of Man - Spirit, Soul, Body.

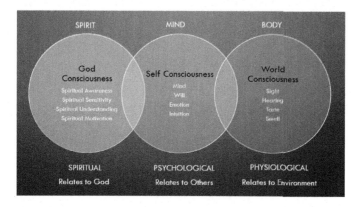

1 Thessalonians 5:23 says *"May your whole spirit, soul, and body be kept blameless at the coming of our Lord Jesus Christ"*. If you are Christian this means to be pure and do good in order to enter the Kingdom of Heaven. If you are a spiritualist, this means you have transcended your ego and within ascension, you have no need or will to judge.

It implies we are a living spirit that has a soul that lives in a body... the 3 parts that make up our whole being. As long as we attend to all 3 parts of who we are, to our best ability, we will transcend.

This next verse holds the key to being successful at attending to our spirit, mind, and body. In the Bible, it says in Thessalonians 5:24, *"The one who calls you is faithful, and he will do it."*

This is to remind us God or source, his spirit, his energy is living in and through you. All that's required to tap into this God energy is intention.

With transmutation or alchemy from an unstable state to a pure state, we can identify where we are unbalanced to balanced.

Instability is seen as chaos when reflected in us so that we can reorder, transform and transmute to bring about progress. When we can see the world as a mirror to ourselves only then can we bring about change within ourselves.

When you see something in another person that causes a negative emotion to arise, look within and ask "What aspect of that behavior do I see in myself?" then ask yourself why it is causing an emotional response. This could be something you should work on in the 1st stage of spiritual alchemy.

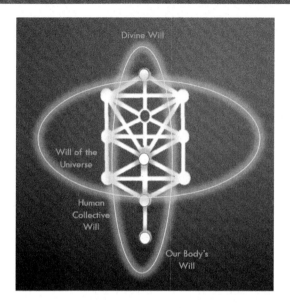

Power of 3 is necessary for the light or spirit to come into the physical where it can transform and evolve. Paracelsus says, "the soul unites the two contraries, the body, and spirit, and changes them into one essence."

The various pillars often correlate with the will. You will see this form demonstrated with masculine and feminine energy making up equilibrium as discussed in Chapter 4, but here the top represents divine will, the center is the will of the universe, the 2nd from the bottom is the human collective will, and the very bottom is our body's will.

Not only are there 3 pillars on the tree of life, but each of those has 3 spheres above the physical. You see, the tree's structure reveals that there are 3 main triads and 3 horizontal cross bars. Only when the 3rd aspect came in could the universe be created, why? Because there must be a source of all light which is represented by the apex of the tree called the crown.

The soul unites the two contraries, the body and spirit, and changes them into one essence."
-Paracelsus

That light must be expanded out just like how you become expansive with your energy body; this outward-reaching force includes the masculine aspect of creation and is the emanation from the source called wisdom.

To bring this energy into formation there must be a 3rd aspect that draws the light inward to be embodied as the

the feminine aspect of creation, called understanding. It completes the upper triad of the 1st sacred geometry of the triangle where the 3 pillars are also established as the rest of the tree is formed according to this original pattern.

What is spirit or light trying to transform into?

In alchemy, you will hear about the Philosopher's Stone.
The Philosopher's stone is an unknown substance called the tincture or the powder that is meant to have the ability to transform base metals into precious metals. From a spiritual point of view, it is the elixir of life...the transformation.

You may hear many definitions of this because alchemy can be applied in many ways. This can be translated into the godlike or perfected human that is a perfectly aligned light body where all aspects of body soul, and spirit have all been transmuted and unified into one immortal being of light.

In Buddhism, this is called the Rainbow Body.

To achieve this our body, mind, and soul must go through the alchemical transformation. If we want to align all three aspects, we must do so through the soul. Side note, the soul is directly connected to God energy.

Why the soul?

The soul is the operating system and the interface that allows our internal spirit to interact with the physical body. The soul mediates the high vibrational energies of the spirit and filters them so that the body can handle and utilize the body at this level, and also to translate and filter the energies on the body back up to the spirit.

Do we realign our soul?

There are many ways to achieve alignment, one method is meditation.

Meditation can be practiced to quiet the mind and find peace within, heal and transform, and remind our soul who we are as a being of love and light.

All healing is self-healing we must go to the depths of our body and soul to heal ourselves. We need to learn the programming language of the soul, and as we ascend the Tree of Life we transcend the soul.

When we realign our soul to spirit, we begin to create a life we are meant to live through love. You begin to release your ego and find joy and grace within. When you embrace these emotions you will notice patterns that lead to the recognition of your life's purpose.

You will repeat the cycle of the powers of above and below.

Our souls' operating systems can become corrupted by unhealed trauma that led to not perceiving ourselves as whole or in oneness anymore. We intuitively know what our minds and bodies need, but sometimes it's easier to do nothing and go with the flow rather than choose again and go in a different direction.

Our mental patterns, emotional attachments, our habits, our subconscious sabotage, or belief systems...all ego-driven blocks to ourselves. We may have had good intentions, but we allowed human conditioning and ego to take the wheel and run ourselves off the road. Often people that are completely unaligned to their life purpose have no idea how they got there. They are either blissfully unaware of the path chosen or in total anguish over the fact that they chose to spend half of their lives distracted..

These indoctrinations corrupt our soul path with things we have learned from the world around us, but they are not true to our spirit. To correct this, we need to purify these belief systems so that there is authenticity and movement. We focus on the outer world, we think the world needs to change and it does indeed, but change has to start from within. The first step and every step afterwards must come from you.

It's time to stop misaligning our souls with things that don't serve us...are you ready for change? If you are, welcome to the beginning of your best life.

CHAPTER 4
Principal of Rhythm

"Everything flows, in and out. Everything has its tides; all things rise and fall. The pendulum swing manifests in everything, the measure of the swing to the right is the measure of the swing to the left & rhythm compensates."

The Principle of Rhythm applies to the Power of 3 - it says all things must rise and flow, and everything is constantly isolated between 2 poles until it finds a balance point...this applies to all realms in mind, matter, or energy.

How do we shift our rhythm to harness this principle?

- Be aware of your cycle and rhythms, know when you are in a flow versus an ebb.
- Learn to not fight it, but rather use it.

How do we achieve equilibrium?

- Bring in equal amounts of discipline and structure on one hand, balanced with creation and intuition on the other.
- Balance masculine and feminine energy aspects of creation.

These correlate with the 3 bars on the Kabbalistic Tree of Life. Here again, we see the Power of 3.

The pillar on the left is called the pillar of form and is seen as feminine, the pillar on the right is seen as the pillar of force and is seen as masculine, and the middle pillar is the pillar of equilibrium which represents and connects the 5 pillars of both masculine and feminine.

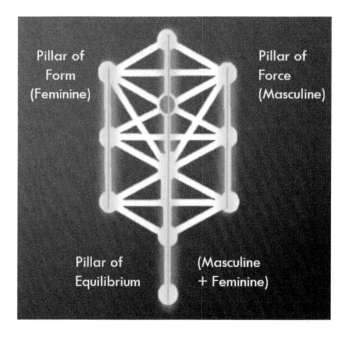

Alchemy says there must be a masculine and feminine aspect combined, the mercury. It takes the union of 2nd, sulfur, and 3rd, salt, to create anything new.

Mercury + Sulfur + Salt

CHAPTER 5
Spagyrics

Spagyrics
To draw out the essence through the process of separating
and re-assembling

At first, these 3 essentials (body, soul, spirit) are bound up together within any material, but then the material gets polluted and corrupted in some way. To perform the alchemy, they must first be extracted and drawn out. From this, they are carefully separated and then purified.

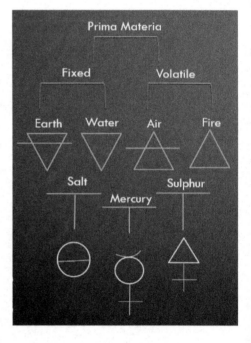

You can see to the right how these 3 essentials draw up to the elements that are either volatile or fixed that is of creation, or oneness with God.

This raises the vibration lifting the body up to spirit while also drawing down the spirit to become more embodied. In this heightened and enlightened state, the 3 purified essentials are then recombined and brought to a stabilized and perfected form.

What are these 3 essentials within us?

Hermes Trismegistus says they are body, soul, and spirit. The Bible and many other sacred books state this as well.

Mercury is the **spirit**, sulfur is the **soul**, and salt is the **body**. In addition, mass is for the **body**, energy for the **soul**, and light for the **spirit.**

By bringing energy, light, or spirit down into material density, the transformational process is necessary.

"The power of it is integral, if it is turned into Earth"
-The Emerald Tablet

CHAPTER 6
Phases of Alchemy

Nigredo	Albedo	Rubedo
dark night of the soul	purification and raising	crystalize or solidify back into a more complete and integrated balanced form

We do all 3 of these phases multiple times in our lives until we become more whole while learning to harness and express ourselves by working with the laws of nature to expand through multiple cycles.

Within the Hermetic Code, alchemy's rich tradition of metaphorical representation, it is noticeable in the three-color scheme: black, white, and red. These three colors represent different spiritual phases at which we find ourselves. At our core approaching enlightenment with imperfect knowledge and then the full glow of wisdom and induction. In Chinese culture, red is a lucky color that symbolizes the spirit, the life force, due to its being the color of blood.

Tied into the Hermetic Code is a parallel symbolism of seven metals (representing the original seven planets) of which lead (Saturn), silver (the moon), and gold (the sun) correspond to black, white, and red.

Nigredo - dark knight of the soul - time of rooting out impurities and imbalances,

Albedo- white phase is a time of purification and raising vibration to connect back to the spirit and then bringing that higher energy back to be embodied in the physical,

Rubedo - the red stage is where we crystalize or solidify back into a more complete and integrated balanced form.

Let's look at how these stages are broken down further:

• CALCINATION – TO CONVERT WITH FIRE
• DISSOLUTION – TO BREAK DOWN
• SEPARATION – TO LET GO
• CONJUCTION – TO JOIN IN UNION
• FERMENTATION – TO CHANGE
• DISTILLATION – TO PURIFY
• COAGULATION – TO MAKE INTO A STRONGER MASS

Don't be surprised if you realize you have already been through most of the stages throughout your life. Some of these you will learn as you go through the stages to varying degrees. The macro level is your overall growth as a soul, whereas the micro level is a result of karmic lessons learned on earth.

You will find that you may go through these alchemical stages simultaneously, even at the macro and micro levels until all your karmic lessons have been learned. The more you experience the more maturity gained and wisdom developed.

As the soul heals and grows through the journey of life you will experience many different life lessons. Some lessons may take lifetimes to understand until you learn the role of the ego on earth.

CHAPTER 7
Nigredo

In the 1st stage of spiritual alchemy, Nigredo, we will focus on the 1st three phases of spiritual alchemy: calcination (convert with fire), dissolution (to break down), and separation (letting go).

Let's talk about the word Nigredo – what does that mean?

Well, it's the blackening – our obstinate dark side, our dark knight of the soul sort to speak.

Three subcategories of Nigredo that will be covered are:

- CALCINATION – TO CONVERT WITH FIRE
- DISSOLUTION – TO BREAK DOWN
- SEPARATION – TO LET GO

Revelations 6: 2-8 from the Bible, New Testament

2 And I saw, and behold a white horse: and he that sat on him had a bow; and a crown was given unto him: and he went forth conquering, and to conquer.

3 And when he had opened the second seal, I heard the second beast say, Come and see.

4 And there went out another horse that was red: and power was given to him that sat thereon to take peace from the earth, and that they should kill one another: and there was given unto him a great sword.

5 And when he had opened the third seal, I heard the third beast say, Come and see. And I beheld, and lo a black horse; and he that sat on him had a pair of balances in his hand.

6 And I heard a voice in the midst of the four beasts say, A measure of wheat for a penny, and three measures of barley for a penny; and see thou hurt not the oil and the wine.

7 And when he had opened the fourth seal, I heard the voice of the fourth beast say, Come and see.

8 And I looked, and behold a pale horse: and his name that sat on him was Death, and Hell followed with him. And power was given unto them over the fourth part of the earth, to kill with sword, and with hunger, and with death, and with the beasts of the earth.

In these verses, the 4 horses of the apocalypse are bringing death by sword, disease, or beast as they usher in the judgment day, notice how each is assigned a color?

Black, pale yellow, white, and red as they represent the Four Greek elements of earth (black), air (yellow), water (white), and fire (red)-. black, white, yellow, and red.

This scheme of four elements belonged to an earlier strand of Alchemy, one predating the birth of Christ, and then in the 15th century the colors were reduced to three and the yellow color was tossed aside. The four original colors symbolize the journey from the darkness of human ignorance to the reddish 'sunlight' of illumination.

Before the sun can shine, the 'death' of the old self must first take place. In Revelation, amidst a story of devastation: the earth is consumed with fire, hail, blood, and smoke. With alchemy, this process occurs on an inner level called calcination (burning) which we will cover soon.

Calcination
To Convert with Fire

In the calcination stage, you are returning to the most organic and original ingredients so that impurities are removed. In alchemy, this is achieved through heat burning the substance down to ash, which is then pulverized using a mortar and pestle and heated again in a crucible. The substance could be plant, animal, or metal.

In spiritual alchemy, we are not burning ourselves literally, instead we are conceptually "burned" and broken down into ashes. We do this by creating insecurities, resentment, self-doubt, and fear which results in depression, anger, and mistrust of our intuition by seeking answers outside ourselves.

The calcination stage is developed at an early age when you were first developing social skills and continued to develop throughout your life because of human conditioning that affects internal change and growth.

As you grow and experience duality you feel the "burn" causing you to deliberately self inflicted conditioning for growth. Some of our hardest experiences result in the most growth. They test our will and challenge, and our beliefs so we have no choice but to expand our soul's capacity to exist through wise, expansive love.

Before you came into your body you had a contract and knew exactly what your lessons would be...you agreed they were the best lessons to expand your soul.

You understood... I need to learn this and that in this lifetime to grow in wisdom at a soul level so I will give myself those family members and that partner. I will give myself this experience at this age, and that will give me enough burden and wounding in life to do the job in hopes you won't "rinse and repeat" in the next lifetime.

You did this because you knew those experiences would result in the right lessons taught by human conditioning that would result in hardship at the perfect times of your life. This also applies to growing through the human ego.

What purposes do the human ego serve?

1. To keep you looking for love outside of yourself
2. To keep you seeking acceptance and approval from others
3. To be important and special through the eyes of others

When you identify that you are trying to control your circumstances or make something happen on your own time instead of God's, or even control something in your mind then you know that there's fear present.

When fear is present you look at a perception of yourself you created to show you were misaligned with a higher power.

Your presence here is when you forget that there is a higher power, that a presence and ever-present energy is supporting us. You get yourself into fear-based thoughts so that you are learning that fear is through reconditioning ego control.

Truly reconditioning our thought processes, reconditioning or belief systems, prayer, meditation any type of spiritual path is really a mental reconditioning of unlearning fear and remembering love.

That's what we are here learning to do...help you unlearn the story you created for yourself and remember love.

We all have fear-based limiting belief systems that have been ingrained in us since childhood. Those beliefs might be created for money, or I'm not good enough, or how could I possibly be worth anything. These belief systems are blocking you from living your absolute best life. You will develop positive and negative internal emotional drivers because of ego-based experiences.

What happens when we create emotional drivers?

REACTION

Reaction in the ways of personal needs, triggers, the little voice in your head chatting away keeping you trapped in deceptive illusions of fear and pain.

The more internal chatter, the more "diseased" our brain becomes until we become close-minded, compartmentalizing, and overthinking everything...most of all taking EVERYTHING personally.

Does this remind you of yourself or someone you know?

Using the example of the Great Phoenix...

Have you heard of the Great Phoenix rising up out of the Ashes?

In the calcination stage, you rise up from your self-created ashes.

The Phoenix is a mythical bird of great beauty set that lives for years in the desert to burn itself so that it can rise out of the Ashes in the freshness of youth just to relive another cycle year after year. It is also a representation of hope.

So, this is the first step to real healing, to witness them without any judgment and to be conscious of how they are making you feel.

Because it comes from a root cause, conditioning comes from a moment in time when we separated from God and love.

You have an experience of separation - you called upon your angels and guides - you cried out and they heard you but when they merged with you the shutdown began. The I want to be in control person that immobilized their energy and ego took control instead of embracing oneness within you, and then continued to build up a world that is a false belief system, and so you continued to re-purpose it.

What really will begin this journey of undoing is the first step, which is crucial because without that willingness, being tired of witnessing and looking at it, we can have the catalyst for change. Are you committed to change?

To create that change, a transformation of a belief system that has held you back for a lifetime requires a spiritual connection, a spiritual awareness.

Through your human conditioning, you rise out of ashes and are born again with a fresh outlook of joy, wisdom, and greater balance.

The processes in these 1st three stages are often referred to as "Dark Night of the Soul" because you are looking within, seeing your truth, looking your skeletons in the closet in the eye, and saying...THAT'S NOT ME, I RELEASE YOU!!

Once you have burned through human conditioning you are ready to start your transformation.

Dissolution
To Break Down

The 2nd stage within Nigredo is Dissolution – to break down, you are breaking down the negative beliefs, the pain, the trauma...all of it. Why? To build it back up...we will talk about that part later, but for now, let's dig deeper within ourselves.

When an alchemist is working with plants, animals or minerals in this stage they use water or acid to break down the ash created in the previous calcination stage. This process prepares for the next stage, separation. We aren't going to do this literally, please know this is figuratively, so no one throw acid or anything else on yourself or animals...only love here, ok?

In the dissolution stage, you must work on breaking down the ego control, releasing patterns that have kept you stuck, moving into self-forgiveness, and starting to see the truth in self-limiting belief systems. This is the hardest stage for most because it's a hard look in the mirror and undo a lifetime of human conditioning. You can't change what you won't acknowledge.

Dissolution of the soul is called a return to innocence, or rebirth. I am not referring to the born-again Christian kind of rebirth, I'm talking about rebirthing yourself mentally and emotionally.

In this stage, you release negative emotions and heal your younger selves to create new patterns of living that promote self-love.

In the dissolution stage, you will expose the ego, any repressed thoughts or belief systems, or patterns and dissolve (release) the false personality also known as human conditioning personality in preparation to start healing.

As you examine pain, resentment, betrayal, and rejection in any way you must ask yourself two questions?

- Is this true?
- How do I know it's true?

Most people can't hold on to negative belief systems once they have been debunked. Sometimes you will hear people say "just let it go", however just letting it go isn't that easy when those beliefs have been drilled deep into your psyche.

You will hear people say, "just forgive" in response to a parent for example that let a bad situation happen to you. That's not going to change your internal programming alone because you can still associate a negative charge or emotion around it.

Choosing to stop running can be scary because the ways we've been running have been the ways that we've saved. There's nothing safe about that, true safety lives in our freedom, emotional freedom.

You must break it down and examine it on a truth and life-purpose level. Once see we are all playing roles to trigger a response in yourself or another person you have no choice but then see the truth behind it.

Here are some examples of emotional triggers due to human conditioning:

- I'm not good enough.
- Everyone hates me.
- I never have enough money.
- Everyone is better than me.
- I'm not deserving enough.

These feelings will keep being triggered until you examine them and break them apart.

Look at yourself in the mirror.

This is you.... brilliant, glorious, perfectly made just as God intended you to be.

Did God make any mistakes?

What do you say to yourself? (Write it down if you want to, this will be helpful as we go through every stage.)

Look at what you wrote or thought of.... does that belief make you worth less or more now? Why?

Notice the story you're in...we will pull each belief out and isolate it.

Now, let's evolve this thought....

- Is this true, can I know this is true that I am _?
- How do you react when you believe that thought? Examine that thought and picture as they come.
- Is it true? No? What can we replace it with?
- This is how you determine it's not for you, can you let this go now that you acknowledge it's not true? (tear it up)
- Can you let this go? Are you going to dredge it up later today or tomorrow? It takes work to hold on to that belief system, right?

Ignorance is the belief in something not true, truth is education. Mind is the cause, life is the effect.

Can you choose love for yourself now? You teach people how to treat you...what do you want them to know about you?

You have three brains: the head brain , the heart brain , and the gut brain. All three are connected.

Head Brain – helps you understand life's lessons and why you developed human conditioning from a logical perspective.

Heart Brain - allows you to go through an internal healing process where you feel love, compassion, and start to nurture the younger versions of you.

Gut Brain - processes the emotions you're ready to release. You begin a process of negative belief systems associated with those younger selves so you can see true beauty in them and you.

As humans, we're only we're always looking for
four things in our lives:
- To be loved and accepted
- To be seen and heard
- To be nurtured
- Be supported

So how did we get from a baby feeling loved, supported, nurtured, etc to full-on ego control?

To answer this we have to consider the 3 rules of the mind to understand we indeed created our reality.

3 Rules of the Mind:
- Your mind does exactly what it thinks you want it to do and what it absolutely believes is in your best interest based on your thoughts, feelings, and beliefs it has registered from your thinking, responses, perception, and interpretation of your life events.
- Your mind only responds to the pictures you make in your head ad the words you say to yourself – and you can change them at any time, but your words become your reality.
- What's negative and familiar, make these unfamiliar by leaving it behind, and what's positive and unfamiliar, make familiar by leaning towards it creating new habits and beliefs.

In life, when we do not get one of these four items, we're desperately looking for them, and often take foolish actions as a result of not receiving them.

Love & Acceptance = Self Forgiveness & Self Acceptance

Focus on your healing, knowing what triggers you, examining reactionary behaviors, understanding this life is a classroom, and acknowledging through understanding we are all uniquely and divinely made, and we all experience human conditioning.

Ego Check

Realize the ego creates self-importance in the eyes of others which keeps us from seeing our own beauty. As you heal every younger version of yourself try to see your experiences as a beautiful life lesson that made you the strong person you are today.

But what made you the strong person you are today? As you see in the boxes below, from the time you were born to age 6 you were in download mode. This is where all that human conditioning started because your core beliefs were hardwired and were held in your subconscious database.

And then from ages 7 to 11 your ego began applying those hardwired beliefs thanks to socialization and full consciousness all the way to adulthood where we added responsibility and moral reasoning.

The brain is hardwired to pay more attention to negative experiences than positive ones, to be alert to danger and pain-both physical and emotional, and to ensure survival.

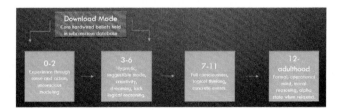

Separation
To Let Go

The 3rd stage within Nigredo is separation- to let go.

From an alchemical point of view, this stage is where you will alchemize the animal, plant, or metal by isolating the desired components in by filtering, cutting, agitating, or setting with air to create a material that is impure to be discarded. What's left is pure and ready for the rest of the alchemical process.

Spiritually, the separation stage is where we separate ego from self. Now don't get me wrong, you can never really 100% remove the ego because we are humans having a human experience. Earlier we talked about duality, without some degree of ego, we would not become conditioned. The point of this exercise is to not be ruled by the ego and instead could view it as an outsider looking in.

As the ego is tamed, we also can identify reactionary behaviors which at this stage should be happening less and less. You will have the innate ability to see the truth by seeing people that play a role are simply there for you to learn a lesson, and therefore there is no need to be a victim.

In this stage of separation, understand that you are not a victim. This is a life you created. You decided on every moment and wrote the code...so see every moment as an opportunity for growth.

Learn to see with the lens of love. See others now moment for what it is. Are you reacting to them? Why? What could have caused their reaction... a bad day, losing their job, the dog died, a car cut them off, sleeping badly because their partner broke up with them last night.

Learn to pause before reacting and accepting for yourself what may not be for you. The more you practice applying this lens the easier it will become until one day you aren't even trying...you just are. You notice things come easier because you are putting out good vibes, and people are reacting to you better because you are just loving them without judgment.

At this stage as you move through separation from ego fully understanding you are the creator of your life experiences, notice how the ego has its own programming.

Our ego has programmed us to perpetually look for love and acceptance outside of ourselves and self-importance. Now that you notice the ego programming, override its power over you.

You will start to notice the programming of the ego first by seeing patterns from younger selves to now.

In this stage become the observer of what's going on inside you internally and externally.

- Are you acting out of need?
- Are you projecting your hurt, fear, and internal injury onto others?
- Are you in victim mode?
- Are you looking outside yourself for love and acceptance?
- Are you trying to be more important to others?

With transmutation or alchemy from an unstable state to a pure state, we can identify where we are unbalanced to balanced.

Instability is seen as chaos when reflected in us so that we can reorder, transform and transmute to bring about progress. When we can see the world as a mirror to ourselves only then can we bring about change within the alchemical process.

CHAPTER 8
Albedo

In the 2nd phase of spiritual alchemy, Albedo, we will focus on the next 3 stages of spiritual alchemy: conjunction- to join in union, fermentation – to change, and distillation- to purify.

Let's talk about the word Albedo – what does that mean?

In spiritual alchemy, the second phase is albedo, the 'whitening' where the soul is washed clean.

This involves a deep look within our human nature, a kind of self-loathing at one's own inferiority. This insight was also known as 'bitter water'.

In Revelations 8:10-11 *"The third angel blew his trumpet, and a great star fell from heaven, blazing like a torch, and it fell on a third of the rivers and on the springs of water.*
The name of the star is wormwood.
A third of the waters became wormwood, and many people died from the water because it had been made bitter."

Of course, this scripture is a metaphor for the arduous journey of the soul as it undergoes purification.

The many who died from the water are initiated into death-rebirth rituals you find within religions, after which arrives a state of purification.

This is symbolized in Revelation 17 promise that *'to him that overcometh ... I give of the hidden manna, and I will give him a white stone, and upon the stone, a new name written, which no one knoweth but he that receiveth it.'*

Even in the Bible, the phrase "Living Water" has been used numerous times to signify redemption, reformation, and renewal of our spiritual life in the Lord. Another point to note is that only rivers and water springs, and that too one-third of them all, are affected by Wormwood. Interestingly, some sources state that Christianity constitutes one-third of the total population of the world! Therefore, the fallen star Wormwood is considered by many as Satan who fell among the nourishing, drinkable waters of the earth (Christ's followers) and killed them through contamination...thus the reason for purification.

Conjunction
To Join in Union

Conjunction describes the action of multiple objects vibrating at the same point in time and space and coming together in balance. On a spiritual level, we are bringing opposite experiences into balance.

Spiritual vibrations are the purest forms of spiritual energy that make up your consciousness. Even has positive & negative mass, but for you, me, and everything else to exist it MUST vibrate. Even your thoughts and actions cause vibrations in the spiritual energy fields. Even our subtle body is made up of spiritual vibrations and frequencies.

In this stage, the alchemist recombines the separated elements left over after the first 3 alchemical stages to produce a new substance by manufacturing out of the opposing elements of fire in the calcination stage, water in the dissolution stage, and air in the separation stage to create a new compound of earth essence in the conjunction phase bringing all elements back into balance.

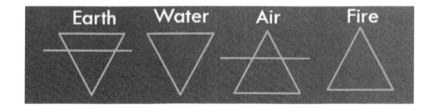

If old fears resurface in this stage, don't worry... you are being provided with two things:

- The opportunity to heal previous conditioning within you at even deeper levels by peeling away more layers.
- The opportunity to resist and oppose patterns that need balancing.

Examples of opposing energies:
- Masculine and feminine energy
- Left and right brain
- Giving and receiving
- Love and hate

Female and male energy must be in balance. If you notice more out-of-balance than in-balance, go back to the Nigredo stage and examine the truths behind those emotions.

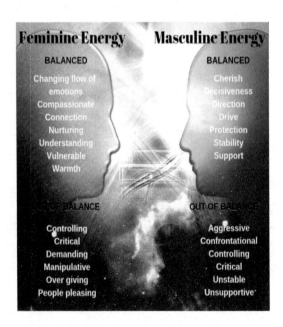

Fermentation
To Change

Stage 5 of the spiritual alchemy process is called fermentation – to change

In traditional alchemy this stage comes after an alchemist has brought together the opposing elements from the 1st three stages of alchemy and has unified these into a new element in the conjunction stage bringing new life forces into the material, he has been cultivating such stage one calcination.

The fermentation stage has two phases: putrefaction and spiritualization.

Putrefaction is where the good material the Alchemist has extracted is left alone to rot and decompose. Most often manure is added to this material to accelerate the rotting process. By adding this to the digesting bacteria it brings new life force into the material which changes the nature of the material until a milky white fluid accumulates on the blackened rotting material.

Spiritization is referred to as the Golden light. Once you have reached the fermentation stage of alchemy you will be in a regenerative, marvelous spot within yourself, finding truth and joy from within all whilst experiencing human conditioning.

Negative people will be very hard for you to be around, and they will naturally drop out of your life because vibrationally you are not an energetic match. You will naturally seek high-vibrational people.

Just as you learn to love yourself and others, embrace this emotion:

- Take the time to recognize truth in situations and people
- Let go of the self-judgment and false beliefs systems
- Acknowledge when the ego is taking over, call it out when it shows up in your life
- Notice the desire for balance in your life, and see value in both masculine in feminine energies

Once you experience this you will naturally ferment, you will rot and ooze...don't judge it. Just stay connected to your higher self.

You will feel anger, want to quit, and sway from any level of change or transformation. Just stick with it and you will find enormous comfort in the new, positive, healthy emotions. Let go of the security blanket called ego and start evolving into the authentic version you were always meant to be.

Examples of self-limiting beliefs created by ego:

- I'm not good enough
- I'm not smart enough
- I'm not pretty enough
- Life is too hard
- I am better than others
- I need others to respect me
- I am defined by power and money
- My unique qualities are unacceptable
- I blame others for my misery
- I need someone else to love me to feel complete
- I need to control others or my surroundings to be important
- I need people to understand, accept, and acknowledge me
- Judgmental of social status
- I'm a victim
- My material belongings define me

How many of you have 1 or more of these beliefs about yourself?

Distillation
To Purify

The 6th stage of spiritual alchemy, also under Phase 2 called Albeto is Distillation...to purify.

In the distillation stage, the substance is boiled to increase the concentration of the pure substance. In this process, any lasting impurities are distilled off. Repeating this process, also called sublimation, which releases the essence of the substance that's transformed to gas, and then condensed into a white powder... thus the reason the distillation stage is often referred to as the white stage of alchemy. This white powder is also what alchemists call the mother of the stone because it is what will give life to the final stone called the philosopher's stone. If you recall in the distillation stage the alchemist ferments the substance so it hardens into a stone before it can be made permanent and is highly concentrated.

From a spiritual alchemy point of view, distillation is a repeated separation and recombination of the different aspects of your personality put in place to check the inflated ego and filter impurities. The mother of the stone describes where your soul will have distilled off both the behaviors that no longer serve in the last remnants of the ego's control as you undergo a rebirth and become prepared for the final stage of alchemy... coagulation.

Through spagyrics we learned to raise our vibration lifting the body up to the spirit while also drawing down the spirit to become more embodied to realign our soul, but how?

There are many ways to achieve alignment, one method is meditation.

Meditation can be practiced to quiet the mind and find peace within, heal and transform, and remind our soul who we are as a being of love and light.

All healing is self-healing....we must go to the depths of our body and soul to heal ourselves. We need to learn the programming language of the soul, and as we ascend the Tree of Life we transcend the soul.

When we realign our soul to spirit, we begin to create a life we love. You begin to release your ego and find joy and grace within. When you embrace these emotions, you will notice patterns that lead to the recognition of your life's purpose.

You will repeat the cycle of the powers of above and below.

Our soul's operating system can become corrupted by unhealed trauma that led to not perceiving ourselves as whole or in oneness anymore. We intuitively know what our minds and bodies need, but sometimes it's easier to do nothing and go with the flow rather than choose again and go in a different direction.

Our mental patterns, our emotional attachments, our habits, our subconscious sabotage, or belief systems...all ego-driven block ourselves. We may have had good intentions, but we allowed human conditioning and ego to take the wheel and run ourselves off the road.

These indoctrinations disrupt our soul path with things we have learned from the world around us, but they are not true to our spirit. To correct this, we need to purify these belief systems so that there is progress. We focus on the outer world, we think the world needs to change...and it does indeed, but change has to start from within.

It's time to stop misaligning our souls with things that don't serve us...are you ready for a change? If you are, welcome to the beginning of your best life.

How do you transmute emotions?

The first step to transmuting the emotion you don't want to feel into a higher frequency is to identify it. What is the emotion you're feeling? Then what is the emotion you would rather feel? What would your life feel like if you chose the opposite of the feeling you're feeling now? If you chose love instead of hate, what would happen? Then what could you do... to turn that feeling around in that moment. What thoughts can you choose? What actions can you take?

Then step 2, is the validation of your emotion. Let your awareness drop into your heart chakra, and let yourself visualize the color of the negative emotion you're feeling. Sit in that emotion for a moment and recognize how the experience feels. As the emotion turns around, let your breath push it outward and exhale the negative emotion color through the heart chakra. Visualize that color being released. Then think about the emotion you'd like to replace it with.

In Step 3, the "choose again" visualization. Imagine the crown chakra at the top of your head is the positive color of your higher frequency emotion, then inhale that positive color and exhale through the mouth the negative color to breathe out that negative emotion and breath in the positive one.

As you inhale the positive color and exhale the negative color, visualize the room filled up with the negative color and then once it's filled and you've let it all outside of you, keep repeating until you visualize the room filled up with the positive color.

And finally step 4, replace past behaviors with thinking &feeling emotions & actions of benevolence, forgiveness, compassion, generosity, and kindness.

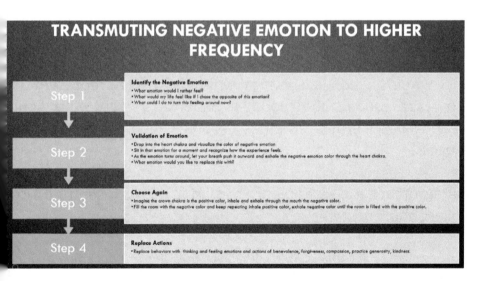

TRANSMUTING NEGATIVE EMOTION TO HIGHER FREQUENCY

Step 1	**Identify the Negative Emotion** • What emotion would I rather feel? • What would my life feel like if I chose the opposite of this emotion? • What could I do to turn this feeling around now?
Step 2	**Validation of Emotion** • Drop into the heart chakra and visualize the color of negative emotion • Sit in that emotion for a moment and recognize how the experience feels. • As the emotion turns around, let your breath push it outward and exhale the negative emotion color through the heart chakra. • What emotion would you like to replace this with?
Step 3	**Choose Again** • Imagine the crown chakra is the positive color, inhale and exhale through the mouth the negative color. • Fill the room with the negative color and keep repeating inhale positive color, exhale negative color until the room is filled with the positive color.
Step 4	**Replace Actions** • Replace behaviors with thinking and feeling emotions and actions of benevolence, forgiveness, compassion, practice generosity, kindness.

CHAPTER 9
Rubedo

Rubedo is often known as the "redness of life" or "the blood"

Let's talk about the word Rubedo – what does that mean?
The Rubedo stage describes the attempt of the alchemist to integrate the psychospiritual outcomes of the process into a coherent sense of self before it is embraced. This stage can take some time to complete due to the needed fusion and corroboration of insights and experiences coming forward.

The symbols used in alchemical writing and art to represent this red stage can include blood, a phoenix, a rose, or a figure wearing red clothes. Countless sources mention a reddening process.

Matter of fact, the seventeenth dictum of the 12th century Turba Philosophorum states:

O Turba of Philosophers and disciples, now hast thou spoken about making into white, but it yet remains to treat concerning the reddening. Know, all ye seekers after this Art, that unless ye whiten, ye cannot make red, because the two natures are nothing other than red and white. Whiten, therefore, the red, and redden the white.

Looking at the picture below this process is visible with the first phase of Nigredo – the black and looking into our own darkness, then albedo- the white, the pureness, and finally Rubedo- the red transcending into oneness.

In the state of whiteness, one doesn't live in the true sense of the word because it needs life or the blood. This experience of transforming us into an ideal state into a 100% human mode of existence by moving the blood into a glorious state of consciousness that completely dissolves the darkness within us. Not even the ego stands a chance.

Then the opus magnum is finished: the human soul is completely integrated. The Rubedo refers to the awakening of now moments, being present but paired with the mind of an evolving and ambitious ego.

The consciousness and subconsciousness have all undergone operations... they cooked, separated, evaporated, remixed, and reproduced. In short, we are fully present and able to navigate full duality with presence and acceptance.

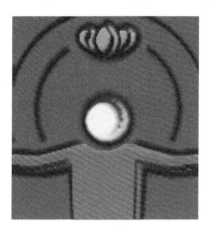

Architype

A collectively-inherited unconscious idea, pattern of thought.

Looking at Rubedo from an archetypal perspective, it represents the Self and is the consummation of the four phases of alchemy, the merging of ego and Self.

It's described the birth of a soul emergence. This phase, Rubedo, indicates a process that cannot be reversed since it involves the struggle of the self toward its manifestation.

The Self manifests itself in "oneness," a point in which a person discovers their true nature, the authentic self, a seeing of oneself in alliance with God. Another interpretation is the "reunification" which entails the power of 3 and the reunion of body, soul, and spirit dissolving all inner conflict.

The Architype's

The word "archetype" was coined by psychologist C. G. Jung who believed there were narrative patterns that exist within the human psyche. An archetype is the core of your personality and is influenced both by your inborn nature and your life experiences. In the next pages, you will find a simplified description of each archetype. You may find that more than one feels like it represents a core part of your personality or identity, however, there is usually one that you will feel perfectly describes you.

Also, your core archetypes can change over your lifetime. Take note if you feel a certain archetype represents who you <u>were</u> versus who you are <u>now</u>. Then, consider if you're hanging on to any of the beliefs from your old archetype, that no longer serve you now.

Which of these archetypes do you feel represents you the most?

What aspects match your personality the strongest?

The Dreamer

Life is for: freedom and happiness
Fear: being punished unfairly, being bad or wrong
Strength: faith and optimism
Weakness: naïve, defensive
AKA: innocent, romantic, utopian, naïve

The Good Neighbor

Life is for: connecting to others, belonging
Fear: being left out, different, standing out, rejected Strength:
empathy, down to earth, peaceful
Weakness: loses one's own self, superficial
KA; good old boy/girl, silent majority

The Hero

Life is for: proving one's worth, courage
Fear: weakness, vulnerability
Strength: competence, courage, boundaries
Weakness: arrogance, always battling, attracts people who
need saving
AKA: warrior, dragon slayer

The Caregiver

Life is for: protect, care for, rescue others
Fear: selfishness and not being needed
Strength: compassion and generosity
Weakness: martyrdom, self-sacrifice, being exploited
AKA: altruist, helper, saint, nurturer

The Explorer

Life is for: freedom to discover yourself through exploring
Fear: getting trapped, conformity, emptiness
Strength: autonomy, independence, ambition, integrity
Weakness: aimless, lack of commitment
AKA: seeker, wanderer, individualist

The Lover

Life is for: intimacy, connection, relationship & being attractive
Fear: being alone, unwanted, unloved
Strength: passion, appreciation, connection
Weakness: people pleasing, losing self in others, dependency, attention seeking
AKA: friend, team-builder

The Rebel

Life is for: breaking rules, revolution or revenge
Fear: powerlessness or complacency
Strength: outrageousness, radical freedom, disrupting status quo
Weakness: crime, conflict, instability
AKA: revolutionary, wild, outlaw

The Creator

Life is for: creating things of enduring value, making visions reality
Fear: mediocrity, settling, the status quo
Strength: imagination, problem solving, action
Weakness: perfectionism, impatience
AKA: artist, inventor, innovator, dreamer

The Jester

Life is for: living in the moment
Fear: being bored or boring others
Strength: joy, levity, play
Weakness: wasting time, irresponsibility
AKA: the fool, practical joker, goof off

The Sage

Life is for: seeking the truth, growth
Fear: ignorance, being duped or misled
Strength: self-reflection, intellect, seeking knowledge
Weakness: studying to excess with no action, over analyzing
AKA: philosopher, advisor, thinker, teacher

The Visionary

Life is for: understanding the laws of the universe, making
things happen
Fear: unintended negative consequences
Strength: following dreams, big picture, future vision, win-win
solutions
Weakness: becoming manipulative
AKA: catalyst, inventor, charismatic leader, medicine man

The Ruler

Life is for: control and power, winning
Fear: chaos, losing control, being controlled
Strength: responsibility, leadership, organization, goal
oriented
Weakness: being authoritarian, unable to delegate
AKA: leader, manager, aristocrat

Coagulation
To Make into a Stronger Mass

The seventh and last stage of alchemy is coagulation. In this stage, the Mother stone becomes the philosopher's stone.

The philosopher's stone is said to be a transmuting agent that is difficult to achieve by alchemists because it could instantly perfect any substance to which it was added and therefore turn lead into gold.

This is a stage where you become a stronger and wiser version of yourself as you learn to be in observance of life and others. You can see truths and spiritual roles in yourself and others more easily, without ego control, without judgment, and maintain your peace within.

"The Tincture"

The Philosopher's stone is an unknown substance, also called "the tincture sought by alchemists is a mythical alchemical substance capable of turning base metals such as mercury into gold or silver. It is also believed that an elixir of life could be obtained from it. It is also called the elixir of life, useful for restoration and for attaining immortality, and at one point in history was the most sought-after goal in alchemy.

The philosophers' stone was the central symbol of alchemy, embodying perfection, enlightenment, and pureness. Efforts to discover the philosopher's stone were known as the Magnum Opus ("Great Work"). Medieval alchemists and mystics believed they were justified in their search for the mythical elixir of life, a universal medicine thought to contain the recipe for the renewal of youth. Self-works through matter (the red area) towards Unity Enlightenment (purple area) with truth & morality of the higher will (yellow area).

The Self manifests itself in "wholeness," a point at which a person discovers their true nature. Another interpretation phrased it as "reunification" which entails the reunion of body, soul, and spirit, leading to a diminished inner conflict.

Focusing on the blue area- this is the make of a man and a woman...a circle. Then a quad triangle, out of this triangle make a circle and now you have the Philosophers Stone

Truth, Love, Good, Right, Morality, Natural Law, Higher Self, Higher Will

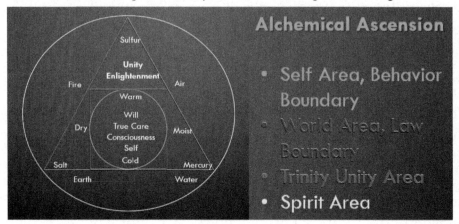

The blue circle is the area of self, consciousness, care and will where harmony is within the consciousness expressions, our inner reality

The red square is reality, nature, matter and the universe that represents the harmony of perceptions with reality, this is also our outer reality.

The purple triangle represents unity enlightenment where we experience the actualization of our true self. This is where we experience harmony with aspects of our higher self and natural law. We know right and wrong, make corrections regarding our truths and heal from it so we can grow and evolve.

Notice the trinities (power of 3 again) of masculine feminine, enlightenment; the mind body and spirit; knowledge, understanding and wisdom; salt (body), mercury (spirit) and sulfur (consciousness) we discussed in a previous chapter?

Then finally on the yellow triangle we have a higher essence of truth and morality, and we begin to react to the will of the spirit leading to life purpose.

CHAPTER 10
Exercises

This chapter is intended to walk you through transforming negative beliefs about yourself and life experiences into positive ones by encouraging inward reflection. This inward reflection serves to show you:

- how you see yourself, and how you have the power to turn it around
- how you see your goals and desires, and how to fine tune them into a life path that brings you pleasure
- how to identify relationships and areas of your life that don't serve you, and how to reflect and grow past them

I encourage you to work through every section of this workbook to completion so that you have come "full circle" by the time you have reached the end.

For more exercises like these please check out my paperback book "Spiritual Coaching Workbook: Don't Be the Only One Getting in Your Way" on Amazon, found in my authors page (Jessica McRae) or contact me at www.therapeutictransformations.org.

Limiting Beliefs

We all have fear based limiting belief systems that have been ingrained in us since childhood that might be created for money, or I'm not good enough, or how could I possibly be worth anything.

These belief systems are blocking you from living your absolute best life.

As humans we're only we're always looking for four things in our lives:
- To be loved and accepted
- To be seen and heard
- To be nurtured
- Be supported

So how did we get from a baby feeling loved, supported, nurtured, etc to full on ego control?

To answer this we have to consider the 3 rules of the mind to understand we indeed created our reality.

Belief systems that are blocking your success in some way.....but guess what....you can change it!

Ego & Fear

What purposes do the human ego serve?
1. To keep you looking for love outside of yourself
2. To keep you seeking acceptance and approval from others
3. To be important and special through the eyes of others

When you identify that you are trying to control your circumstances, or make something happen on your own time instead of God's... or even controlling something in your mind then you know that there's fear present.

When fear is present...you look at a perception of yourself you created to show you were misaligned with a higher power.

Your presence here is when you forget that there is a higher power, that there is a presence and ever present energy supporting us. You get yourself into fear based thoughts so that you are learning that fear is through reconditioning. Reconditioning ego control.

Truly reconditioning our thought processes, reconditioning or belief systems, prayer, meditation any type of spiritual path is really a mental reconditioning of unlearning fear and remembering love.

That's what we are here learning to do...help you unlearn the story you created for yourself and remember love.

3 Rules of the Mind

#1

Your mind does exactly what it thinks you want it to do and what it absolutely believes is in your best interest based on your thoughts, feelings and beliefs it has registered from your thinking, responses, perception and interpretation of your life events.

#2

Your mind only responds to the pictures you make in your head ad the words you say to yourself – and you can change them at any time, but your words become your reality.

#3

What's negative and familiar, make these unfamiliar by leaving it behind, and what's positive and unfamiliar, make familiar by leaning towards it creating new habits and beliefs.

LOVE & ACCEPTANCE = SELF FORGIVENESS & SELF ACCEPTANCE

Self Limiting Belief Examples

- I'm not good enough
- I'm not smart enough
- I'm not pretty enough
- Life is too hard
- I am better than others
- I need others to respect me
- I am defined by power and money
- My unique qualities are unacceptable
- I blame others for my misery
- I need someone else to love me to feel complete
- I need to control others or my surroundings to be important
- I need people to understand, accept, and acknowledge me
- Judgmental of social status
- I'm a victim
- My material belongings define me

Practice
Growth Mindset

Select your favorite affirmations from the list below and put them somewhere you will see them every day

Challenges, risks, and failures do not reflect that I am a failure, they are opportunities for me to grow and improve.

I care more about the process and the journey and who I become along the way than I do about the outcome.

What other people think about me is none of my business.

I am always looking for the meaning and lessons contained in all situations that can help me fulfill the greater purpose in my life.

I move past the discomfort of making mistakes quickly because I learn the lesson and allow it to help me improve so I can do better next time.

I am the master of my thoughts, emotions, and actions and I do not give my power away by reacting to others criticism, judgment, or actions in a negative way.

I was made perfectly as I should be, God doesn't make mistakes.

If my talents, abilities, and intelligence are not fixed, this means my potential is truly limitless!

Reframe Your Thoughts

The Power of Interpretation (Perspective)
Your interpretation of events either empower you or disempower you. Even the worst experiences of life, that feel like a curse, can be re-framed to find the silver lining or blessing contained within them.

It is the MEANING we attach to a situation that determines whether it moves us forward or holds us back. The meaning also impacts the way we react and feel about any circumstance.

Find the Silver Lining
For every seemingly negative circumstance in life, there either was (or could be) a positive outcome because of it.

You can choose to interpret events in a way that is disempowering, or you can interpret them in a way that is empowering by asking yourself:

"What else might be going on here?"

What did I learn from this experience?"

"What can I do differently next time?"

"What positive outcome eventually came as a result of this situation?"

Printed in Great Britain
by Amazon

26938269R00046